The Preschooler's BUSY BOOK

Trish Kuffner

Meadowbrook Press

ISBN 978-0-88166-561-1 (Meadowbrook)

Executive Editor: Megan McGinnis
Editor: Alicia Ester
Production Manager: Paul Woods
Creative Director: Tamara JM Peterson
Cover Illustrations: Dorothy Stott
Interior Illustrations: Laurel Aiello

Published by:
    Meadowbrook Press
    5451 Smetana Drive
    Minnetonka, MN 55343

www.meadowbrookpress.com

Printed in the United States of America

Dedication

For my husband, Wayne, and our five precious children, Andria, Emily, Joshua, Johanna, and Samuel.

I have learned far more from you than you will ever learn from me.

Contents

Introduction

If I Had My Child to Raise Over Again
If I had my child to raise over again,
I'd fingerpaint more and point the finger less.
I'd do less correcting and more connecting.
I'd take my eyes off my watch, and watch with my eyes.
I would care to know less and know to care more.
I'd take more hikes and fly more kites.
I'd stop playing serious, and seriously play.
I'd run through more fields and gaze at more stars.
I'd do more hugging and less tugging.
I would be firm less often, and affirm much more.
I'd build self-esteem first, and the house later.
I'd teach less about the love of power, and more
   about the power of love.

—*Diane Loomans*

Although coping with the needs of a baby can be tough for new parents, it usually doesn't take long for most to feel comfortable with changing, feeding, holding, and rocking their infants. As babies grow into toddlers, most parents are able to cope with wiping noses and behinds, making meals no one eats, finding toys and clothes and sticky finger marks everywhere, and, of course, doing laundry, laundry, laundry. But as children leave the toddler stage and become full-fledged preschoolers, their needs change dramatically. Few parents feel prepared to meet the daily demands of life with a preschooler, and most find it a constant challenge to meet their physical, mental, emotional, and spiritual needs.

I first encountered life with a preschooler during an exceptionally rainy, coastal Canadian winter. Andria, my oldest daughter, was three. Her sister, Emily, was almost two, and baby Joshua was not yet six months old. Emily was in the midst of toilet training, and Josh nursed at least every two hours. Andria, normally sweet-tempered and easy-to-please, was becoming difficult. As the rain continued, her moodiness increased. She needed new things to do, new experiences to stimulate her, but most of my time and energy went into meeting the needs of the two younger children. As the days dragged on, and our frustration festered, I entertained a multitude of doubts about my ability (or lack thereof) to be a good mother. I had always heard about "quality time" with your child; I seemed to have an awful lot of quantity time without much quality!

While I knew I couldn't always expect to drop everything to get involved with her, I knew there must be something I could do to provide my preschooler with a more creative and stimulating environment. I knew there must be activities that would both challenge and entertain her. I wanted ideas for little projects we could work on together, but I also wanted things she could do on her own while I was busy elsewhere. Since we were living on one income, I also needed activities that made use of basic items we already had around the house.

I started to reorganize our home to better meet the changing needs of our family. I began collecting and saving all kinds of interesting things that we could use in our activities. I became much more organized and tried to plan for special things we could do together. I also relaxed a little and learned to enjoy my children and their small and simple pleasures. Confidence in my parenting abilities returned as I began to feel in control again.

While I don't claim to be a "specialist" of any sort, my experiences at home, all day, every day, with three very young children, taught me much about what works and what doesn't. This book is a compilation of the ideas and activities that met my needs as a parent, as well as the needs of my children, during those challenging preschool years. It contains suggestions for every situation and occasion, for both indoors and out, for summer and winter, for quiet times and not-so-quiet times. Although this book is written by a stay-at-home mom as a resource for others in the same situation, be assured that it is well-suited for anyone who has a preschooler in their life: mothers or fathers, grandparents, aunts or uncles, babysitters, daycare workers, preschool teachers, church workers, or playgroup leaders. If you are looking for one good book on what to do with a preschooler and how to do it, this book is indeed for you.

While many ideas in this book may continue to entertain your children long after the preschool stage, the activities in this book are most suitable for children between the ages of three and six. Because abilities of children in that age range vary greatly, some ideas will be too advanced for a three-year-old, and some will be too simple for a five- or six-year-old. Use your judgment in choosing activities that best meet the capabilities and interests of your child, and be prepared to supervise when necessary.

Enjoy your preschooler! Although it may seem at times that they will never grow up, they always do. The long, seemingly endless days will gradually be replaced by days with not enough hours in them. Children who once needed you for everything will need you less and less, and the days of leisurely walks, playdough and afternoon naps will be a warm and fuzzy memory. My hope is that both you and your child will have many happy hours of playing, growing, and learning together.

Trish Kuffner

P.S. A note on the use of "his" and "her"; in recognition of the fact that children do indeed come in both genders, and in an effort to represent each, the use of the male and female pronouns will alternate with each chapter.

Chapter 1
Rainy Day Play

"The years rush past, as every older woman will tell the young mothers who complain that they still have two little ones at home and it seems like forever before they will all be in school. Oh no, they say, time flies—enjoy them while they're young—they grow up so fast....

The mothers agree that indeed the years do fly. It's the days that don't. The hours, minutes of a single day sometimes just stop. And a mother finds herself standing in the middle of a room wondering. Wondering. Years fly. Of course they do. But a mother can gag on a day."

—*Jain Sherrard*

Life with preschoolers can be a wonderful, rewarding experience. On long, warm, summer days, when adults and children alike can be outside from sunup to sundown, parenting can seem very fun and easy. But "fun" and "easy" are not words you are likely to hear from anyone who has endured a week of rain with several house-bound preschoolers. Most preschoolers have a great amount of energy, but a relatively short attention span. Boredom can cause acutely irritating behavior in small children and should be avoided as much as possible. Now is the time for big, messy art projects (see Chapter 7) and marathon baking sessions.

Invite friends for lunch frequently, and always be prepared with something fun for the children to do indoors. Some of the activities that follow require a table or countertop, and some require water—these are best-suited to your kitchen. Other water-related activities are a natural for the bathroom and bathtime. The rest are more flexible, and can be easily adapted to the bedroom, living room, family room, or other room in the house that has plenty of floor space and an absence of breakables.

Clean Coins

Old toothbrush
Soap
Water
Bowl
Coins
Dishcloth or paper towel
Salt and vinegar (optional)

Your child can practice cleaning coins with an old toothbrush and some soap and water. Fill a bowl with a small amount of water and place a few coins in the bowl. Your child will have fun brushing the coins with soap to make them look brand new. When the coins are as clean as your child can make them, dry them with a dishcloth or paper towel.

For super-shiny coins, mix a small amount of salt and vinegar in a bowl. Drop the coins in and watch the tarnish fade. (If you do use vinegar, make sure your child does not get any in her eyes; soap is bad enough, but vinegar will really sting!)

Bath Paints

This game is an all-time favorite with our children, but merits a few words of caution. If you have ceramic tile in your bathtub area, you may want to skip this one, as the food coloring may stain the grout. If your child has sensitive skin, the shaving cream (depending on the brand) can cause irritation. In any case, children will almost certainly need another bath after this activity!

Shaving cream
Food coloring
Muffin tin
Spoon
Paintbrushes or sponge

Squirt shaving cream into the individual sections of a muffin tin. Add a few drops of food coloring to each section and mix with a spoon. The kids will love painting the walls, the tub, and themselves with their hands, a sponge, or paintbrushes. Older children will enjoy mixing the colors to create new ones. Clean up is easy when the fun ends—just hose down the tub, with your child in it!

Indoor Sandbox

Cardboard box or plastic baby bath
Puffed wheat or rice cereal
Sandbox toys

Create an indoor sandbox by filling a cardboard box or plastic baby bath or basin with inexpensive puffed wheat or rice cereal. Use buckets, shovels, and dump trucks, or measuring cups, spoons, and bowls. (Uncooked rice can be inexpensive when bought in bulk, and it makes an interesting road surface for small trucks or other wheeled toys.)

Paper Punch

Hole punch
Paper scraps

Give your child a hole punch and scraps of paper in various colors. She will amuse herself for quite some time making confetti that can be saved and used for arts and crafts activities.

Listening Game

Have your child close her eyes and guess the sounds you make. Use household objects, such as keys, coins, silverware, or a whistle. Tap on a pot with a spoon, snap your fingers, or click your tongue.

Nail Board

Nails
Wooden board
Hammer
String or elastic bands

Hammer nails into a piece of board. Allow your child to create a design by wrapping string or colored elastic bands around the nails. Hammer the nails in a pattern, or use rows or circles so your child can create her own designs. Make sure that the nails only penetrate the top side of the board, put away the hammer and excess nails, and supervise your child to avoid accidents.

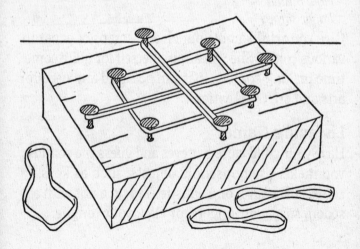

Magnet Magic

Refrigerator magnets
Heavy paper

Give your child a couple of refrigerator magnets and a piece of heavy paper. Place the paper between the two magnets and show your child how to move the top magnet by moving the bottom magnet. On the top side of the paper draw a road or some other pattern for your child to follow.

Lid Art

Plastic lids from gallon milk jugs
Glue
Paper plate or piece of cardboard

If you buy milk or juice in gallon plastic jugs, save the small plastic lids. Once you have a collection of different-colored lids, let your child glue them onto a piece of cardboard or a paper plate to create a design. Kids will also have fun sorting lids by color, lining them up end to end, creating patterns, or using them as play money.

I Love You Because . . .

Paper and pen
Crayons or markers

Ask your child, "Why do you love Daddy?" Write her responses on a sheet of plain or construction paper, and have your child decorate it with crayons or markers. Place the "love note" as a surprise in Dad's lunch the next day. You can vary the questions you ask your child, such as, "What's the funniest thing Daddy ever did?" Or do this for friends or grandparents and other relatives. Some of the answers you get may be priceless!

Living Room Picnic

Tablecloth
Picnic dishes
Picnic food
Summer clothing

Brighten the coldest, rainiest, or stormiest of days by having an indoor picnic. Spread a tablecloth on the floor of your living room and use outdoor dishes or paper plates. Picnic-type dress (shorts or bathing suits) is essential, and don't forget your sunglasses.

Newspaper Golf

Newspaper
Tape
Golf or tennis balls
Masking tape or paper

Make golf clubs for each player by rolling up several sheets of newspaper and taping them securely. Lay down a sheet of paper or use masking tape to mark several "holes" on the floor or carpet. Use your golf club to try to hit (roll) the ball to the hole. Reward the winner (the first to hit the ball to the hole) with a raisin, chocolate chip, or other small treat.

Carpet Raceway

Books or scraps of wood
Matchbox cars or other toys with wheels

Make a raceway or train track on a carpet by laying down books of equal thickness side by side to make a smooth lane, or use pieces of plywood or two-by-fours. (Your raceway can be any length and can be straight or have turns.) This will transform the carpet into a smooth surface for racing toys with wheels.

Balancing Board

Board measuring about 8 inches wide by 6 feet long
Magazines or books

Place a board across two piles of magazines or
books (books will be less slippery than glossy
magazines). Have your child practice keeping her
balance by walking across the board. As your child
grows more steady, you can place one end on a
chair and she can walk up it, or place it across two
chairs as she grows even more bold. Remember:
The higher you build the balance beam, the more
supervision your child will need.

Go Fish

Stick for fishing pole
String
Magnet
Scissors
Construction paper
Glue or tape
Metal paper clips

Cut fish shapes out of construction paper. Glue or tape metal paper clips to the back of each fish. Make a fishing pole out of a long stick and a length of string. Tie a magnet on the end of the string. Go fishing. This works well if you place the "fish" on the floor and let your child dangle her line over the back of the couch. You can also use this game to help your child learn her basic skills: Draw a shape or write a letter or number on the back of each fish, and have her identify it when caught.

Little Carpenter

Golf tees
Styrofoam
Toy hammer

Give your child some golf tees, a toy hammer, and a piece of Styrofoam. She can hammer the golf tees into the foam in a design, or just hammer for the sake of hammering.

Chapter 2
Kids in the Kitchen

"You cannot teach a child to take care of himself unless you let him try to take care of himself. He will make mistakes; and out of these mistakes will come his wisdom."

—Francis Bacon

Work and play are inseparable for kids; your work is very often your child's play. Whether you are in the kitchen a little or a lot, your child will naturally want to be with you. The kitchen is a tantalizing place for children, full of wonderful things to smell, touch, and taste. Anyone who has ever watched a small child eat will know that, to a child, food is as much a toy as it is a nourishment. Children, even as young as two, will enjoy making their own peanut butter sandwiches, and most will agree that finger Jell-O is one of the best foods ever invented! Make sure your child's hands are clean, accept that things may get a little messy, and let your child enjoy his food experience.

With a little bit of effort and a lot of patience on your part, the kitchen can also become a wonderful classroom for your child. Talk to him about the magic of the kitchen, how yeast or baking powder makes things rise, how the batter baked in the oven turns into a cake, or how cornstarch thickens a sauce. He will want to help you measure and mix, wash vegetables, cut out cookies, and sift dry ingredients. Include him in your work, and take the time to teach him as you cook.

Make or buy your child his own recipe box and fill it with his favorite recipes, written with simple words and illustrated with pictures and symbols. Include some simple "no-cook" recipes that he can make with little supervision. Remember to always be safety-conscious. Make sure any dangerous objects are well out of reach, and be sure to closely supervise any use of sharp utensils, the oven, or stove, or, better yet, make a rule that only an adult can use those things.

Taste Testing
Blindfold
Various food items

Blindfold your child and have him identify by taste
and smell some of his favorite foods (ice cream,
pickles, yogurt, cereal, cookies, and so on). Have
him describe the different tastes and textures and
ask him to group them as sweet, salty, bitter, sour,
spicy, or tangy.

Homemade Peanut Butter
Peanuts in the shell
Food processor
Baby food jar (optional)
Decorative fabric and ribbon (optional)

Shelling enough peanuts to make a little peanut
butter is sure to keep your child busy. Place the
shelled peanuts in your food processor and grind
until smooth. Store in a covered container. To give
as a gift, place the peanut butter in a small baby
food jar with lid. Cover the lid with a circle of fabric, and tie a ribbon around the neck of the jar to
keep the fabric in place.

Popcorn Ball Creatures

Ingredients

¾ cup sugar
½ cup water
1 teaspoon white vinegar
¼ teaspoon salt
¾ cup brown sugar
¾ cup butter
½ cup light corn syrup
8 cups popped popcorn

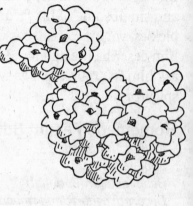

Materials

Medium saucepan
Candy thermometer
Large bowl
Wax paper

1. Stir all ingredients except popcorn and butter in a medium saucepan over medium heat until the mixture reaches 260 degrees on a candy thermometer (hard ball stage).
2. Reduce temperature to low; add butter.
3. Put popcorn in a large bowl. Pour the mixture over it, coating the popcorn. Cool slightly.
4. Butter your child's hands and let him mold the popcorn into animal shapes. Place the shapes on wax paper until ready to eat.

Apple Shapes

Apples
Knife
Metal cookie cutters

Peel apples and cut them into thin slices. Give your child small metal cookie cutters and let him cut shapes out of the slices.

Chase the Pepper

Pie plate or small sink
Pepper
Bar of soap
Sugar

Your child will love to show off this neat trick. Fill a pie plate or small sink with water. Shake pepper on the water and dip a piece of wet soap into it. The pepper will run away from the soap. Now shake some sugar into the clear area and the pepper will run back.

Flour Drawing

Cookie sheet
Flour

Lightly sprinkle the surface of a cookie sheet with flour. Show your child how to draw in it with his finger. Or draw a letter, number, or shape in the flour with your finger and have him draw the same next to yours.

Happy-Face Sandwich

Bread
Peanut butter
Raisins or chocolate chips
Knife

Spread peanut butter on one side of a piece of bread. Have your child decorate it with eyes, a nose, and a big, happy smile made of raisins or chocolate chips.

Chapter 3
Outdoor Adventures

"Any adult who spends even fifteen minutes with a child outdoors finds himself drawn back to his own childhood, like Alice falling down the rabbit hole."
—*Sharon MacLatchie*

Children of all ages have such an endless amount of energy. Outdoor play, every day, in almost any weather, is essential. Most children are as happy all bundled up for the snow as they are in shorts in the summertime. Rain provides countless opportunities for play, whether walking beneath an umbrella or stomping in the puddles, and a brisk walk is appropriate almost anytime. Playing outdoors in all types of weather is great fun for kids. You should encourage your child's outdoor play every day, and join her whenever you can.

The following suggestions will provide your preschooler with some fun and interesting things to do outdoors. Most activities require a minimum of materials, and you will find that by making slight adaptations, most are suitable for any season and any weather.

Sandpaper Play
Sandpaper
Wood scraps
Glue (optional)
Paint or markers (optional)

Give your child a piece of sandpaper and some small wood scraps. Show her how to sand the wood, and talk about the difference between rough and well-sanded textures. Sanded scraps of wood can be glued together to create wood sculptures and painted or decorated with markers. To avoid splinters, you may want your child to wear gloves for this activity.

Mining for Gold
Small rocks
Gold or silver spray paint

Spray some small rocks with gold or silver spray paint to resemble gold or silver nuggets. Bury the nuggets in the dirt in your yard or sandbox, give your child a shovel, and have her dig for buried treasure. Give younger children some directions, like cold or hot, so they don't get too frustrated. Give older children a treasure map to follow.

Mud Painting

Paintbrush
Mud

In a bucket or other container, mix water with
some clean dirt or earth (without stones, grass,
glass, or any other particles); keep the mud thin.
Give your child a paintbrush and have her dip it
into the mud and draw pictures or write words on
the sidewalk. Be prepared: She will most likely use
herself as a canvas as well! Your child will have fun
hosing her creations off later, or you can leave them
for the next rainfall.

Backyard Camping

Tent
Sleeping bags
Pillows
Flashlight
Snack

You don't have to go far to give your preschooler the outdoor experience. On a fine summer night, set up your tent in the backyard. For children, there is something almost magical about walking in the dark, so go for a walk: listen to night noises and look at stars. If a backyard bonfire is not allowed in your neighborhood, have a snack and a sing-along by the light of a flashlight before you pile into your sleeping bags for the night.

If your child is too scared to spend a whole night outdoors, limit the activity to the walk, and then pile into the house for hot cocoa.

Slip and Slide

Garbage bags or a large sheet of plastic
Liquid dishwashing detergent
Hose or sprinkler

This is great fun for a hot day. Spread out a large sheet of plastic or a few plastic garbage bags that have been cut open to lie flat. Pour a little bit of liquid dishwashing detergent on the plastic, then turn the hose or sprinkler on it. Your kids will have great fun getting a running start then sliding on the plastic. This works great at the foot of a slide or on a gentle slope. Make sure to remove any rocks or other sharp objects from under the plastic.

Kickball

All the balls you can find

Gather together all the balls you can find in your house: tennis balls, soccer balls, basketballs, beach balls, and so on. Line them up one foot apart and have your child kick each one. See which one is the easiest to kick, which one goes the farthest, which one goes the highest, and so on.

Chapter 4
Out and About

"I suppose there must be in every mother's life the inevitable moment when she has to take two small children shopping in one big store."
—*Shirley Jackson*

Children naturally have the desire and the energy to play all the time, but there are times when your child will just have to sit. It may be a long ride in the car, or at the doctor's, dentist's or hairdresser's, or while you wait for your meal to arrive in a restaurant. No matter where you are or what you do, be prepared with quick, easy activities that require a minimum of props to keep a cranky child busy and calm, and a parent sane.

Guessing Bag

Pillowcase or drawstring bag
Small, unbreakable household objects

Place a variety of small, unbreakable household
objects inside a bag. Close the bag so the objects
are not visible. Have your child feel the objects
through the bag and guess what they are.

What Am I?

Make up riddles about animals, objects, or people
for your child to solve. For an elephant you could
say, "I am very large; I have a long trunk; I live in
Africa. What am I?" For a fire truck, you may say,
"I am big and red; I have a loud siren; I help put out
fires. What am I?" Describe people by what they do
(doctors, nurses, police officers), or friends and
family by how they look (tall, wears glasses, long
hair). Be specific to help your child solve the riddle
without getting too frustrated.

Beep

Choose a familiar story, song, or rhyme that your child has heard often. Read or recite the story, song, or rhyme, but substitute wrong words or names in obvious places. For example: "Old MacDonald had a car" or "Mary had a little dog." Have your child listen for the incorrect words and say "Beep!" when he hears one.

Silly Questions

Ask your child silly questions to help him use his imagination and make choices. For example: "Would you rather be a bird or a cow? Why?" or "Would you rather be a table or a chair? Why?" Take turns asking the questions and giving the answers.

Felt Doll

Felt
Pen or marker
Cardboard
Glue
Scissors
Scraps of yarn and fabric
Shoebox

Draw the shape of a person on a square of felt. The person should have clearly defined arms and legs, with the arms held away from the body. Glue the felt to a piece of cardboard and cut out the doll. Glue on yarn for hair, and draw a face with a marker. To make clothing for the doll, place the doll on scraps of fabric and use a marker to trace around the body. Cut out the clothes and dress the doll; the cloth will stick to the doll's felt body. Store the doll and clothes in a shoebox and take the box with you on long car rides.

Edible Necklace

Shoestring licorice
Cereal or crackers with holes in the middle

Tie a knot at one end of a piece of shoestring licorice (or a plain piece of string). Show your child how to thread cereal or crackers with holes in them on the string, and then tie both ends together into a knot. The end result will amuse your child for quite some time. In the grocery store, he can eat one piece each time you put something in the cart; in the car, he can eat one piece each time he sees a dog or a red car.

Fun with Words

Ask your child to tell you what certain words mean to him. Pick out everyday words that he has likely heard before. Some suggestions to get you started: concrete, marriage, retire, divorce, bachelor, anniversary, occasion, special, obedient, country. You may be surprised to find that some of the words in your child's vocabulary are something of a mystery to him. Some of the answers you get will be priceless; write them down for posterity!

Chapter 5
Reading, Writing,
'Rithmetic, and More

" ... children must be ready to learn from the first day of school. And of course, preparing children for school is a historic responsibility of parents."
—*George Bush*

Parents have few responsibilities more important or more rewarding than helping their child to learn. As a parent, you are your child's first and most important teacher. Children generally learn what adults around them value, and you can use your daily activities to informally teach your children about reading, math, and geography, among other things. Children are naturally curious, and there is much you can do to advance their knowledge in these academic areas. The activities in this chapter will help you provide opportunities for your child to understand the connection between academic knowledge and the skills you use every day at home and at work.

READING READINESS

During the preschool years, children develop at an extraordinary rate. Each day's experiences, however familiar to adults, can be fresh and exciting to curious preschoolers. Although your child's incessant curiosity may be aggravating, especially at the end of a long day, it provides an opportunity for you to help her connect daily experiences with words. Tying language to the world your child knows allows her to go beyond that world to explore new ideas. Not only do parents have abundant opportunities to help children develop language, but these opportunities often occur naturally and easily.

While connecting experience to language is an important foundation for learning to read, no activity is more important for preparing your child to succeed as a reader than reading aloud together. When you read to your children, they almost automatically learn about written language. They learn that the words in a particular written story are always in the same order and on the same page. They may also learn that print goes from left to right, that words are made up of letters, that each letter has at least two forms (capital and small) and that there are spaces between words.

Take your child to the library on a regular basis. (Our children receive their very own library cards when they can print their name.) Help your child find her way around the library, and show her how to look for books by her (or your) favorite authors. I recommend *The Read-Aloud Handbook* by Jim Trelease (4th edition, Penguin Books, 1995), or *Honey for a Child's Heart* by Gladys Hunt (3rd edition, Zondervan, 1989). These books offer lots of great reading suggestions for children of all ages.

While reading with your child, you will often have opportunities to answer her questions about the names, sounds, and shapes of letters. Preschoolers are very observant and often focus on company trademarks and logos that include or resemble letters of the alphabet. For example, the golden arches at McDonald's look like an M; pointing that out may be an easy way to begin. Television programs like Sesame Street also may help your child learn letters and the sounds they represent. Try to watch these shows with your child so you can talk to her about the letters on the screen and point out all the other places those letters appear.

Research has shown that children who know the names and sounds of letters when they enter school learn to read sooner. The following activities will help your preschooler learn to identify letters, sounds, and words.

Alphabet Match-Up

Clothespins
Paper
Tape
Pen or marker
Old magazines
Scissors

Write the letters of the alphabet on small pieces of paper and tape them to clothespins, or print the letters right on the clothespins. Cut out magazine pictures, one for each letter of the alphabet, and have your child match the clothespin letters to the beginning sounds of the objects in the pictures. Clip the clothespins to the corresponding pictures.

I See A-B-C

While on a walk, in the car, or at the grocery store, look for objects beginning with each letter of the alphabet. If you like, make this a competition, and whoever gets to the end of the alphabet first, wins. Of course, let your child win at least some of the time!

X's and O's

Paper
Pen, marker, or crayons

Print one letter at the top and center of a sheet of paper. Below this, write many letters of the alphabet in no particular pattern, spreading them over the sheet of paper. Have your child circle the letters that match the one printed at the top. Have her place an "X" over the ones that do not match. For a variation, use pictures cut from old magazines and have your child identify the pictures that begin with the letter you have written.

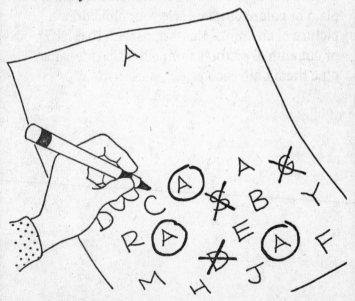

Dictionary Zoo

There is a delightful book called Alfred's Alphabet
   Walk by Victoria Chess *(Greenwillow Books, 1979)*
   that would nicely complement this activity.
Small notebook or loose sheets of paper
Crayons or markers
Old magazines
Scissors
Glue

This is a good rainy day project that can be
completed during one or more sittings. Help
your child print a letter of the alphabet on each
page of a small notebook, or use loose sheets of
plain or colored paper. Have your child draw a
picture of an animal that begins with that letter,
or cut animal pictures from old magazines and
glue them onto each page.

MATHEMATICS

When you think about math, you probably think
"arithmetic"— the adding, subtracting, multiply-
ing, and dividing you did when you first started
school. The truth is that mathematics, the subject
that incorporates numbers, shapes, patterns, estimation, and measurement, is much broader than
that. Although we may not always realize it, math
is everywhere, all around us, present in our world
all the time—in the workplace, in our homes, and
in life in general. Math is a very important skill,
one we all need in our technological world, as well
as in our everyday lives. Encourage your children
to think of themselves as mathematicians who can
reason and solve problems.

The good news is that most children enter
school with the skills they need to succeed in math.
They are curious about quantities, patterns, and
shapes. In many respects, they are natural problem
solvers. You can help build your child's math confidence without being an expert yourself. You can instill
an interest in math in your child by doing math
together—by asking questions that evoke thinking
in terms of numbers and amounts and playing
games that deal with such things as logic, reason,
estimation, direction, classification, and time.

Teach your child that math is a part of the real world. Shopping, traveling, gardening, meal planning, cooking, eating, even laundry are all opportunities that allow you to apply math to your daily routine. Many activities throughout this book deal with cooking, sorting, patterns, and so on. Use them, as well as the following activities, as a fun way to help your child develop her math skills.

One, Two, Buckle My Shoe

This rhyme will help your child's counting skills.
Try showing her objects in groups of one, two,
three, and so on, as you recite the rhyme together.

One, two, buckle my shoe;
Three, four, close the door;
Five, six, pick up sticks;
Seven, eight, lay them straight;
Nine, ten, a big fat hen.

Counting

Give your child household counting assignments.
Have her count all the doorknobs in the house,
or all the cans in the kitchen cupboard, or all the
knives, forks, and spoons in the silverware drawer.
You can adapt this game for outside by counting
cars as you go for a walk, birds that fly by as you
play on the swings, and so on.

Food Count

Empty egg carton
Pen or marker
Small food items (raisins, cereal, chocolate chips, candies)

Write the numbers 1 to 12 on the individual sections of an egg carton. Have your child count out each number using small food items. Then have her fill the numbered section with the correct number of items. Once the sections are filled, work in reverse, having your child identify each number, count the pieces, then eat them!

Calendar Math

Calendar
Markers or stickers (optional)

Read the calendar with your child every day.
Include the weekday name, the month name, the
date of the month, and the year. For example, you
may say, "Today is Tuesday. That means yesterday
was _____ (Monday), and tomorrow will be
_____(Wednesday)," or "Today is the 10th of
March. That means yesterday was the ____(9th),
and tomorrow will be the ____(11th)." If possible,
allow your child to place a sticker on, or mark off,
each day as it is read.

Thirty Days Has September

Teach your child this rhyme about the number of
days in each month:

Thirty days has September,
April, June, and November.
All the rest have thirty-one,
Save February, which alone,
Has twenty-eight and one day more,
We add to it one year in four.

GEOGRAPHY

Geography is the study of the earth, divided into five major themes: location (where it is); place (what makes a place special, both physically and culturally); interaction (between people and the environment); movement (of people, products, and information); and regions (areas defined by distinctive characteristics). Geography is a way of thinking, asking questions, observing, and appreciating the world around us.

You can help your child develop an interest in geography by providing interesting activities for her, and by prompting her to ask questions about her surroundings. To help you think geographically, and to help your child build precise mental images, try to use basic geographical terms whenever possible, i.e., west or north, climate, highway, river, and desert. Expose your child to lots of maps and let her see you use maps regularly.

The following activities are only a few examples of the many ways children learn geography. They are informal and easy to do, and are designed to help you find ways to include geographic thinking in your child's early experiences.

Play City

Markers
Large sheet of paper

Using markers on a large sheet of paper, draw an imaginary city big enough for your child's cars and trucks. Be sure to include some landmarks familiar to your child: bank, grocery store, gas station, park, hospital, school, post office, train tracks, and so on. Tape the finished city to the floor so your child can travel around the city with her cars, trucks, dolls, and fire engines. For a more permanent city, use paints on strong cardboard or wood. Glue milk cartons or small boxes onto the map to make buildings. For a variation, make an imaginary airport or farm.

North, South, East, West
Small toy, book, or household object

Show your child north, south, east, and west by using your home as a reference point. If your child's bedroom faces east, point out the sun rising in the morning. Show the sunset through a window facing west. Once your child has her directional bearings, hide a small toy or household object somewhere in the house. Give directions to its location: two steps to the north, three steps west, and so on.

My Neighborhood

Take a walk around your neighborhood and look at what makes it unique. Point out differences from and similarities to other places. Can your child distinguish various types of homes and shops? Look at the buildings and talk about their uses. Are there features built to conform with the weather or topography? Do the shapes of some buildings indicate how they were used in the past or how they are used now? These observations help children understand the character of a place.

Treasure Hunt

Paper
Pens or markers
Small toys or other treats

Have a treasure hunt in the park, on the beach, in your backyard, or in your house. Draw a map that leads to the treasure, which can be several small toys, cars, or other items.

Litter Patrol

Disposing of waste is a problem of geographic dimensions.

Bag for litter
Gloves
Stick with pointed end

Go on a neighborhood litter patrol with your child. You may want to wear gloves and use a stick with a pointed end to pick up the litter. Talk about litter, garbage, and recycling and how we can help control and take care of our surroundings.

Chapter 6
Music, Dance, and Drama

"The events of childhood do not pass, but repeat themselves like seasons of the year."

—Eleanor Farjeon

Music, dance, and drama are an essential part of our children's general education. Through the study of music, dance, and drama, children acquire knowledge, skills, and attitudes that influence them throughout their lives. In addition to learning music for its own sake, children learn coordination, goal-setting, concentration, and cooperation. Dance activities also offer many benefits for children, encouraging mental and emotional development while enhancing motor skills. Drama involves mind, body, and imagination, and is essential to a child's full development.

This chapter provides simple ideas that will help you stimulate your child's development in these three areas. The following activities will cultivate your child's sense of rhythm, allow your child to experience movement as it relates to music and rhythm, and encourage your child in creative play.

Pie Plate Tambourine

Aluminum pie plate
Hammer and nail
6 to 8 flattened bottle caps
String

Using a hammer and nail, an adult should make six to eight holes around the edge of an aluminum pie plate, and one hole in the center of the same number of flattened bottle caps. Let your child pull a piece of string through each bottle cap and thread it through a hole in the pie plate. Tie a knot tight enough to hold the bottle cap in place, but allow enough slack so that the cap can move freely and hit the pie plate when shaken. Attach each cap in this way; shake to play.

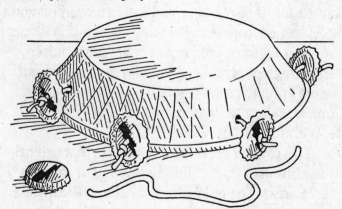

Noise Blower

Empty cardboard tube (toilet paper or paper towel rolls)
Wax paper
Elastic band
Crayons, markers, ribbon, stickers, fabric, construction
*　paper, and other items for decoration*

Cover one end of a cardboard tube with a piece of wax paper, using an elastic band to hold the wax paper in place. Blow and hum into the uncovered end to make a vibrating sound. Older children can make this for themselves, decorating the tube with crayons, markers, stickers, scraps of ribbon, fabric, or construction paper.

Exercise Class

Pretend to have an exercise class in your living room. You can dress in exercise wear if you like, and take turns being the "instructor." Include both locomotor movements (walking, running, jumping, skipping, and so on) and nonlocomotor movements (bending, stretching, twisting, swinging, and so on). Vary the size, level, and direction of these basics to allow your child to discover a large number of movements that can be combined to form basic dance steps. You can also make a point to include these movements in other games you play, such as Simon Says.

Tickle Trunk

Empty trunk or large box
Adult clothes and props

You can encourage your child's dramatic play by
setting up a Tickle Trunk full of props for him.
Fill a trunk or box with adult clothes, shoes, hats,
scarves, gloves, and costume jewelry to use for
dress-up. Old suits are great, as are Hawaiian shirts,
vests, baseball hats, wigs, boots, and slippers (for
girls, include old bridesmaid dresses, costume jewelry, nightgowns, and purses). Great items can be
found at garage sales or local thrift shops. A Tickle
Trunk will be an invaluable part of your child's
dramatic play and items can be added for years.

Barber Shop

Brushes
Combs
Empty hair spray bottle filled with water
Shaving cream
Popsicle stick or old credit card
Towel

Help your child set up a pretend barber shop. Give him brushes, combs, an empty hair spray bottle filled with water, and shaving cream. A wooden Popsicle stick or an old credit card can be used as a razor. Use a towel to wipe off shaving cream and water. Take turns being the barber.

Restaurant

Tablecloth or other linens
Vase with flowers or other centerpiece
Candle (optional)
Menu

Use table linens, flowers (real or other) in a vase, and a candle to set up a pretend restaurant. Take the customer's coat, show him to his seat, give him a menu, and let him order lunch or dinner. Take turns being the waiter and the customer.

Sandpaper Blocks
2 4-inch pieces of a two-by-four piece of wood
Sandpaper
Glue

Glue sandpaper onto the wood, and rub together for an interesting sound.

Moving Questions

Ask your child questions like, "How many ways can you balance yourself besides standing?" and "How many different ways can you move your head (arms, leg, upper body)?" Such questions will help your child become aware of his body and its relationship to other people and the environment.

Chapter 7
Arts and Crafts

"The parents exist to teach the child, but they must also learn what the child has to teach them; and the child has a very great deal to teach them."

—*Arnold Bennett*

Arts and crafts projects provide great opportunities for creative play for your child. Through her work with arts and crafts, your child will learn to think creatively and develop skills in drawing, painting, designing, and crafting. Well-chosen arts and crafts projects will help your child develop concentration and coordination, as well as organizational and manipulative skills. They will promote a sense of great achievement, and are fun and exciting for children of all ages.

That said, one of the main problems I've always had with arts and crafts projects is what to do with all the wonderful things your child so busily and happily creates? Children can produce an enormous volume of work in a short amount of time. Multiply that by two or three children, and you can have a major problem on your hands! Here are some ideas that might help:

- Always be on the alert for creative ways to use your child's art, i.e., as gifts or gift wrap
- Display your child's art around the house, not just on the refrigerator. Visit an art framing shop and ask them to save their mat scraps for you. You may get some pieces that are great for either mounting or framing your child's work.
- Make a calendar of your child's art for Grandma or other relatives. Save your little artist's work throughout the year. As the new year approaches, visit local businesses and collect free calendars. Glue your child's art onto the picture part of each month, so a new masterpiece will be displayed each time the calendar changes.
- Create a "portfolio" for your child. Using a three-ring binder and plastic page protectors, save some of your child's outstanding creations. Be sure to date or write your child's age on each work of art. For extra-large or 3-D projects, take a photo or two and put those in the binder. (The project itself will have to go eventually!)

When the day comes (and it will) to get rid of some of the pictures and projects your child has created, be sure to do it in a sensitive way. Chances are she will not miss the picture that was hanging on the refrigerator for a month, but finding it crumpled up in the kitchen waste basket is sure to make her feel that you don't really value her work. Take items directly to the outdoor trash containers just before the garbage is picked up to save you and your child some heartache.

Old phone books come in very handy for children's little projects. When your child is coloring, painting, or gluing, open the phone book and place your child's paper on a clean page. Then simply turn the page for a clean working surface for the next project. This way, you won't have to worry about finding scrap paper to line your child's workspace, and you won't have to clean paint and glue off your kitchen table nearly as often.

Here are some activities you can use to introduce your child to the world of art. Remember that your attitudes make strong impressions on your child; encourage her to experiment. Arts and crafts projects are a form of self-expression, and your child should know that there is no right or wrong way to create art.

DRAWING

Drawing is probably the first art form your child will experience. It allows your child to express herself creatively and helps the development of her small muscles and hand/eye coordination. Drawing is simple and it can be done anywhere and at anytime. It is something most of us do, in some form or another, all our lives.

Give your child a little variety in her drawing tools and materials. Try using pens, pencil crayons, chalk, and markers. For drawing paper, use construction paper, newspaper, fine sandpaper, or cut-open grocery bags in varying sizes. Your child will also enjoy drawing and tracing shapes, such as circles, triangles, and stars cut from different types of paper.

Crayon Rubbings

Paper or cut-open grocery bags
Small textured objects
Crayons

Place paper or cut-open grocery bags over textured objects, such as leaves, string, doilies, paper clips, fabric, tiles, coins, cardboard shapes, or bricks. Have your child rub a crayon on the paper. Shift the paper and use different colors for interesting patterns.

Self-Portraits

Very large sheet of newsprint or other paper
Markers, crayons, or paint

Have your child lie down on the floor on the paper. Trace around her, then let her fill in the details with markers, crayons, or paint. Tell her to be as detailed as possible: What is her hair like? What color are her eyes? What clothes is she wearing? When finished, hang her portrait in her room or on her door where she can admire it.

Nature Colors

Plants and flowers collected on a walk
Crayons
Paper

Go on a walk with your child, and bring home a variety of plants and flowers, such as grass, leaves, dandelions, and so on. Spread them out on a table in your backyard and encourage your child to draw a picture using only crayons in colors that match the items you have collected.

Wet Chalk Drawings

6 tablespoons sugar
¼ cup water
Colored chalk
Paper, white

Mix together sugar and water and pour over the chalk; let soak for ten minutes. Have your child use the wet chalk to draw on white paper. If you use white chalk, draw on colored paper.

Secret Messages

White crayon or wax candle
Paper, white
Tempera paints
Paintbrush

Use a white crayon or wax candle to write a message or draw a picture on a piece of white paper. Your child can then paint over the paper with tempera paint to see the picture or message appear.

PAINTING

Painting is a wonderful outlet for a child's creativity. Large pieces of paper, pots of paint in vivid colors, big paintbrushes, and a painter's smock will keep your little artist happy on many a rainy afternoon. Provide a good work space, keep supplies handy, and make cleanup part of the project. Work outdoors when you can, and let nature provide further inspiration.

The best kind of paint for young children is poster paint, also known as tempera paint, which you can buy at any art store in premixed liquid form or as a powder that must be mixed with water. You can also make your own poster paint using the recipes in the Appendix. Children rarely need more than three colors: red, blue, and yellow. Teach your child how to mix these colors to create others. Tempera blocks are also available; they are practical because they don't have to be diluted and can't be spilled, making cleanup easier. In addition, tempera blocks are economical, since they are less expensive and last a very long time; however, your child will probably not find them as fun as the slick liquid paints.

Paper can be purchased from an art supply store, but consider some of the following alternatives. Newsprint is a wonderful paper for painting; roll-ends can be purchased cheaply from a newspaper publisher. Visit your local printer and ask if you can leave an empty box for a week or two; she may agree to fill it with all kinds of wonderful paper that would otherwise be discarded. Try fine sandpaper as an alternative art paper for a wonderful effect. For fingerpainting, use the shiny side of freezer paper that can be purchased at the grocery store. It is much cheaper than special fingerpaint paper and works just as well.

String up a line in the laundry room or kitchen to hang paintings to dry. Wet artwork can be attached to the line with clothespins. When dry, be sure to display your child's paintings prominently. And think of creative uses for some of her work; many painting projects make wonderful gift wrap or greeting cards.

Starch Painting

Bowl
Liquid starch
Liquid detergent
Paper or plastic cloth
Powdered tempera paint

Mix a small amount of detergent with liquid starch in a bowl and pour the mixture onto a painting surface, such as a tabletop, paper, or plastic cloth. Sprinkle powdered tempera paint over the starch, and let your child experiment with mixing colors.

Dipping

Paper towel
Bowls of diluted food coloring or strong watercolors

Have your child fold a piece of paper towel into a fairly small packet. Have her dip each corner of the packet into a bowl of colored dye (diluted food coloring or strong watercolors). Use a different color for each corner. Unfold the paper towel and hang to dry. You can use various types of paper; the more absorbent the paper, the faster the dye will spread. Dipped rice paper makes a nice gift wrap, but it is fairly expensive.

Paint Blot Art

Construction paper
Tempera paint, liquid
Spoon
Rolling pin

Fold a piece of construction paper in half like a greeting card, then open it up. Using liquid tempera paints and a spoon, have your child drop different colors onto one of the inside halves of the paper. Fold the paper again with the paint on the inside, and have your child roll a rolling pin over the paper to spread the paint. Open the paper and have your child use her imagination to decide what the blot looks like. When the paint is dry, fold the paper so the paint is on the outside. Use as a unique greeting card.

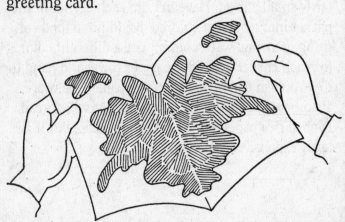

PRINTMAKING

Young children can experience a sense of great accomplishment with printmaking. Not only is printmaking fun, but it allows a young child to achieve an attractive reproduction of an object without a great amount of artistic skill or coordination. Through the repetition of an impression, children can develop an appreciation of texture and design.

Printmaking involves making an impression of an object onto paper or another surface. The object to be printed can be covered in paint using a brush or a paint roller, dipped into paint, or pressed on a print pad.

A print pad can be made by padding up newspaper and soaking it in liquid tempera. Or place a thin sponge in a shallow tray or small bowl and cover it with several tablespoons of paint. For some printmaking, a rubber stamp pad can also be used. To cushion the print, place a newspaper under the paper on which the impression is to be made.

Many different types of paper can be used for printing; newsprint, construction paper, and cut-open brown paper bags are some of the cheaper options. As with many of the painting projects in this chapter, you can use these printing activities to create some great, environmentally friendly gift wrap.

Gadget Printing

½-inch softwood cubes or matchboxes
Small objects in interesting shapes (matchsticks, string, wood chips, curtain rings, bottle caps, or cardboard shapes)
Glue
Print pad or rubber stamp pad
Paper

Glue interesting shapes onto half-inch softwood cubes or matchboxes; matchsticks, string, wood chips, curtain rings, keys, bottle caps, or shapes cut from cardboard are just a few examples. You can make letter or number stamps on wood cubes by drawing the image in reverse, then chipping away the surface except for the shape to be printed. Or use larger objects, such as a potato masher, fly swatter, or salt shaker. Press the object onto the print pad or rubber stamp pad and stamp it on the paper, varying colors and objects to create unique designs.

Sponge Printing

Scissors
Small thick sponges
Clothespins
Print pad
Paper

Cut sponges into various shapes. On the top of each sponge cut two slots for clothespins, making the slots about a quarter-inch deep and three-quarter-inches apart. Clip the clothespins to the top of the sponges for handles. Press the sponges onto the print pad and stamp them onto the paper. Use various shapes and colors for an interesting effect.

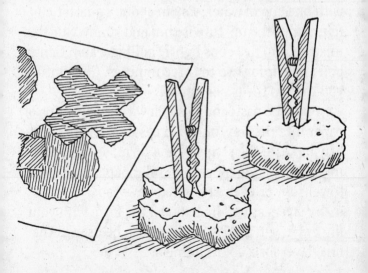

PAPIER-MÂCHÉ

Papier-mâché can be a very messy activity, but it is a lot of fun for children and adults alike. Papier-mâché is a special kind of paper modeling that uses paste in combination with paper or other materials, such as newsprint, paper toweling, gift wrap, crepe paper, tissue paper, construction paper, or aluminum foil. Paper can be torn into two-inch or larger squares or long strips. Torn edges glue better and result in a more interesting finished appearance.

For young children, a basic flour-and-water paste is the best bonding material to use. Begin with one cup of water; mix in about a quarter cup of flour, until the mixture is thin and runny. Stir this mixture into five cups lightly boiling water. Gently boil and stir for two to three minutes. Cool until you can dip the paper into it.

Pour the paste into a shallow tray. Dip strips of paper into the tray, or brush paste on with a paint-brush. Paste the strips over a form, such as an inflated balloon, an empty toilet paper or paper towel roll, or even crumpled newspaper. Add as many layers as you like; model the form with your fingers as you go. Tissue paper can be used as the final layer for a colorful finish.

Papier-Mâché Hat

Papier-mâché paste
2 large squares of wrapping paper
String
Paint

To make a fancy hat, paste together two big squares of wrapping paper with papier-mâché paste. Set this on your child's head, mold the crown of the hat, and tie a string around your child's forehead to hold the shape. After ten minutes, remove the hat, shape, let dry, and paint.

Papier-Mâché Piñata

Large inflated balloon
String
Newsprint or other paper
Papier-mâché paste
Small toys and candy
Crepe paper or tissue paper
Paints

This is a great project to make for a birthday party or other special occasion. Hang a big balloon from a string and cover it with many layers of paper and paste, leaving a hole about six inches in diameter at the top of the balloon, around the string. This will take several days to dry. When dry, pop the balloon and pour in toys and candy, then cover the opening with more paper and paste. Let dry again, then decorate the outside with fringed crepe paper or paints. Have the children try to break the piñata by taking turns swinging at it with a toy baseball bat or golf club.

CUTTING AND PASTING

Most young children gain enormous pleasure from the use of scissors and the feel of paste. Buy your child a good pair of child-safe scissors and teach her how to use them safely. Show her how to keep the edges sharp by cutting sandpaper.

For paste, you can use commercial white glue or make glue or paste using the recipes in the Appendix. Glue and paste is best applied with a small paintbrush, although Popsicle sticks or plastic applicators from the art store can also be used. For variety, tint the glue with food coloring.

Keep a stack of old magazines and catalogs on hand for cutting. An old wallpaper book is also great for all the interesting shapes and patterns it contains. Cut out circles, squares, rectangles, triangles, or other creative shapes, and glue them onto construction paper to make designs and pictures.

Personal Puzzle

Old magazines, catalogs, or greeting cards
Photograph of your child (optional)
Cardboard
Glue
Scissors

Cut out pictures from magazines, catalogs, or greeting cards, or use an enlarged photograph of your child. Glue the picture onto a piece of cardboard that has been cut to the same size. When dry, let your child cut the picture into pieces to create her own puzzle. Puzzles are great for helping your child recognize shapes—a prerequisite to learning letters and numbers.

Gingerbread People

Thin cardboard or brown construction paper
Pen or marker
Scissors
Glue
Lace, ribbon, fabric scraps
Pieces of cereal, small candy, or licorice

Draw the outline of a gingerbread girl or boy on thin cardboard or brown construction paper. Your child can cut it out and dress it by gluing bits of lace and ribbon or scraps of fabric onto the figure. Make a face out of cereal or candy.

Chinese Lantern
Construction paper
Scissors
Glue or stapler

Fold construction paper in half lengthwise and show your child how to cut from the folded edge to within one and a half inches of the opposite side. When cuts have been made along the entire length of the paper, unfold and form into a cylinder by joining together the short uncut ends of the paper. Glue or staple another strip of construction paper for a handle.

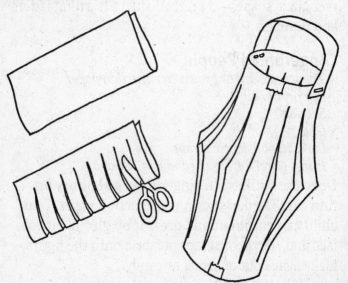

Funny Face

Old magazines
Scissors
Paper
Glue

Look through old magazines, searching for pictures of faces, and cut out as many eyes, noses, mouths, ears, and heads of hair as you can find. Mix them up and have your child piece together a funny face; then paste it onto a piece of paper.

Picture Place Mat

Family photographs
Cardboard or construction paper
Glue
Clear contact paper

Give your child the family photographs that didn't make it into your photo album. Have her glue them onto a piece of cardboard or construction paper and cover with clear contact paper. This place mat makes a great gift for Daddy, grandparents, and other family members.

CRAFTS AND OTHER FUN THINGS TO MAKE

Not only will craft projects challenge your child's imagination and artistic ability, they will fill in many hours on a rainy afternoon and help keep your child stimulated and happy. Make crafts as gifts for friends and family, or use them to brighten up your child's room and the rest of the house. Most of these projects can be made using objects found around the house or collected on your daily walks.

Noodle Necklace
Macaroni noodles
String
Tempera paints
Paintbrush

Make a noodle necklace by threading macaroni noodles on a string. Knot the ends together and paint the noodles with tempera paints. Let the necklace dry thoroughly before letting your child wear her creation.

Rock Art

Rocks
Glue
Paint
Paintbrush
Playdough or fabric scraps, ribbon, or lace

Make rock people or rock animals by gluing together rocks you have collected on walks. Your child can then paint her rock art and add accessories made out of playdough or fabric scraps, ribbon, or lace.

Styrofoam People

Styrofoam balls and blocks in different sizes
Toothpicks
Scraps of yarn and fabric
Glue
Markers or paint

Use toothpicks to join Styrofoam shapes together to form people, a snowman, animals, and so on. Glue scraps of yarn and fabric onto the Styrofoam to make hair and clothes. Use markers or paint to add faces or other details.

Feather Headband

Construction paper or poster board
Scissors
Stapler
Glue
Feathers (optional)
Markers or crayons (optional)

Cut a strip of brown construction paper or poster board about one and a half inches wide. Measure the length by placing the headband around your child's head and stapling the ends together to fit snugly. Cut several feather shapes out of colored construction paper (or gather some real feathers on a walk) and glue to the headband. Your child can draw a design on the headband with markers or crayons if she wishes.

Toy Boats

Styrofoam meat trays
Straw
White construction paper
Scissors
Tape

Make toy sailboats with clean Styrofoam meat trays. Insert a straw into the tray for the mast. Cut triangular sails from white construction paper and tape to the straw. Your child can sail her boat in a bathtub, a swimming pool, or a tub of water.

Modern Art

Piece of cardboard or paper plate
Glue or paste
Small household items (cereal, buttons, macaroni, sequins, cut-up straws, plastic jug lids, and so on)

Give your child a strong piece of cardboard or a paper plate, some glue, and small items of different sizes, shapes, and textures: cereal, buttons, macaroni, sequins, cut-up straws, plastic juice jug lids, and so on. Let your child create her own version of modern art.

Chapter 8
Birthdays and Holidays

"The first holiday may have been invented to celebrate fertility or planting or harvest, but we're sure a mother was behind it. Even then she must have known that nothing could cure her day-to-day drudgery as well as a holiday or brighten the eye of a small child so quickly."

—*Marguerite Kelly and Elia Parsons*

Nothing can disrupt your daily routine like a holiday, yet nothing is quite so important. Mothers and small children alike often need the lift of a special day on which we can focus energy and attention. In addition to celebrating birthdays and traditional holidays, make the most of each small victory and accomplishment. You don't have to go all out all the time; put a candle on the dinner table and use your best china to make even an ordinary day extraordinary. Most of the fun and excitement comes from the anticipation that builds as the celebration draws near, so be sure to allow your child to take part in the planning and preparation for each festivity.

Birthday Time Capsule

Envelope
Writing paper
Pen

This is a wonderful tradition for young and old alike. Each birthday person prepares information to be put into their "time capsule." Ask questions of young children and write down their responses. You may want to ask about favorite foods, songs, activities, friends, and so on. Ask what your child looks forward to over the year, and what he expects life to be like next year on his birthday. When everything is written down, place the paper in an envelope labeled with the birthday person's name and the Date to be Opened (next year's birthday). You'll all have a lot of fun when the time capsule is opened.

Valentine Place Mat

Valentines your child has received
Construction paper or light cardboard
Glue or paste
Clear contact paper

Have your child glue his favorite valentines onto a large piece of construction paper or light cardboard. Cover this collage with clear contact paper to make a place mat.

Heart People

Construction paper in red, white, and pink
Glue or paste

Using red, white, and pink construction paper, trace and cut hearts, ranging in size from two to six inches. Glue the hearts together in different combinations to form heart people, using large hearts for heads and bodies, smaller ones for arms, legs, and so on. You can also try making heart animals.

Valentine Chain

Construction paper in red, white, and pink
Glue or paste

Cut strips of red, white, and pink construction paper, three to four inches long and one-half to one-inch wide. Give the strips to your child and have him form a circle with one strip, gluing the ends together. Take the next strip and loop it through the first circle, again gluing the ends together. Tell your child to make a chain as long as he wants. Use it to decorate doorways, walls, and so on.

Hide the Shamrock

While this game works best with a few children, you can still play when there's just the two of you.

Green construction paper
Scissors

Cut a shamrock out of green construction paper. Choose a child to be "it." While other children hide their eyes, "it" hides the shamrock within a designated area. Everyone then opens their eyes and tries to find the shamrock. The finder gets to be "it" for the next round.

Easter Bunny Mask

Paper plate
Scissors
Pink construction paper
Glue
Pink or white pipe cleaners
Yarn
Hole punch

Turn a paper plate into a bunny mask. Hold the plate against your child's face and mark where the eyes and nose holes should be. Cut out the holes for the eyes and nose. Cut out bunny ears from pink construction paper and glue to the plate. Use pipe cleaners for whiskers. Punch a hole on each side of the plate, and attach two pieces of yarn on both sides to tie the mask onto your little bunny's head.

Easter Grass

Large Easter basket
Pan, large enough to hold the basket
Wheat seeds (about 1 pound)
Vermiculite (about 1 pound)
Plastic wrap

Grow a miniature meadow right in your own Easter basket. About a week before Easter, line a large Easter basket with plastic wrap and fill with vermiculite up to two inches below the rim. Sprinkle the wheat seeds on top of the vermiculite, set the basket in the sink, and add water until the seed bed is moist. You won't have to water it again before Easter. Set the basket in a pan and place it in filtered sunlight. Cover loosely with plastic wrap to keep moist; remove the plastic after two days. The wheat will begin to sprout during the next few days, and by Easter morning, you will have real Easter grass for hiding your Easter eggs.

United States Flag

As you work to make this United States flag for
Independence Day, tell your child what the colors
and shapes represent.

Red and blue paper
Scissors
Glue
Large white paper
Star stickers
Dowel
Tape

Help your child tear or cut a large blue square
and strips of red paper. Glue the strips and square
onto white paper to make a flag. Stick stars on the
blue square. Tape the flag to a dowel and fly the
flag proudly!

Baked Pumpkin Seeds

Pumpkin seeds
Cookie sheet
Salt

As you prepare your Thanksgiving or Halloween
pumpkin, save and dry the seeds. Spread dried
seeds on a cookie sheet, salt, and quickly broil them
until lightly browned. Have your child count them
into groups of two, three, four, and so on, before
eating them.

Pom-Pom Spider

Black yarn
Small square of cardboard
Scissors
Black pipe cleaners
Googly eyes (optional)
Red construction paper (optional)
Glue (optional)

Wind black yarn around a small square of cardboard, top to bottom, until the cardboard is very heavily and snugly covered. Tie a small piece of yarn securely around the middle of the yarn and the cardboard. (This piece should be tied fairly tightly, but not knotted, as it will be tightened after the cardboard is removed.) Using scissors, cut the yarn horizontally at both ends of the cardboard. Remove the cardboard, then tighten and knot the piece of yarn in the middle; it now forms the center of the pom-pom. Insert three pipe cleaners into the knotted center, and bend to form legs. You may have to trim the yarn to form a nice, even ball. Glue on googly eyes, if you like, or cut eyes out of red construction paper and glue them onto the pom-pom. Use thread or yarn to hang your spider from the doorway or in the window.

Glowing Pumpkin Drawing

Construction paper
Orange and black crayons
Black (or other contrasting color) tempera paint and brush
Varnish (optional)

Using crayons, help your child draw an outline of a pumpkin on a piece of construction or other paper. He should press hard, and fill in the outline with plenty of thick coloring. Then have him paint the picture with black (or other contrasting color) tempera paint. Since wax repels water, the colored areas will resist the paint and the painting will "glow." For a really dramatic effect, use fluorescent crayons, and finish with a coat of varnish.

Paper Plate Turkey

Paper plate
Brown paint or crayon
Construction paper in various colors
Glue or paste
Markers or crayons

Have your child color a paper plate with brown paint or crayons. Cut feathers out of colored construction paper, and glue them to the edge of the plate. Cut out a head, a neck, and feet, and glue them to the plate. Draw a turkey face with markers or crayons.

Thanksgiving Tree

Construction paper in fall colors
Poster board or cardboard
Scissors
Markers
Glue or paste
Old catalogs or magazines (optional)

Cut leaf shapes out of colored construction paper. You can draw the shapes on paper and have your child cut them out, or make a leaf pattern your child can trace himself. Draw a tree trunk and branches on a piece of cardboard or poster board. Ask your child to name things for which he is thankful and write them on each leaf (or use pictures cut from old magazines or catalogs). Have your child glue the leaves or pictures onto the branches. Display the tree in a prominent place as a reminder of your many blessings.

Glitter Balls

Styrofoam balls in various sizes
Glue
Glitter
Small shallow dish
Thread

Pour glitter into a shallow dish. Spread glue evenly over a Styrofoam ball, then roll it in glitter. Allow the ball to dry, then attach a thread for hanging on the Christmas tree.

Christmas Countdown

25 small candy canes, individual pieces of
candy, or candy kisses (for each child)
1 bowl, candy dish, or empty coffee can
(for each child)

Place twenty-five small candy canes, kisses, or other
special candy treats into a bowl, candy dish, or
empty coffee can. Beginning December 1, let your
child have one treat from his bowl every day. When
he begins to ask "How many days 'til Christmas?"
(and he will!) he can see for himself by counting the
number of candies left in the bowl.

Paper Plate Wreath

Green paper plate
Red and green tissue paper
Ribbon bow
Scissors
Glue

Cut a hole in the center of a green paper plate. Cut
or tear red and green tissue paper into small pieces.
Have your child twist the paper or crumple it into
small balls and glue them onto the plate. Add a
ribbon bow in a contrasting color.

Graham Wafer House

This "gingerbread" house is made with graham wafers and is easier for little hands than one made with traditional gingerbread.

Graham wafers
Cardboard milk carton
Ornamental Frosting (see Appendix)
Gumdrops, candy, raisins, chocolate chips,
    LifeSavers, cereal, and other edible decorations

Make Ornamental Frosting to hold the house together. Use the frosting to cement graham wafers to the sides of a cardboard milk carton (remember to cover the frosting with a damp cloth when you're not using it). Allow the frosting to set partially before adding the roof. Decorate with gumdrops, candies, raisins, chocolate chips, LifeSavers, cereal, and so on.

Christmas Card Puzzles

Old Christmas cards
Heavy paper or cardboard
Glue
Scissors

Glue Christmas cards onto heavy paper or cardboard. When dry, cut into puzzles. The puzzle can be very simple and consist of only one card, or it can be more complicated, with two or more cards overlapping to make patterns and designs.

Kwanzaa Flag

The significant colors of Kwanzaa are black, red, and green: Black symbolizes the color of the people, red their continuing struggle, and green their hope for the future.

Paper
Red, green, and black crayons or markers

Divide a piece of drawing paper horizontally into three equal parts (either by drawing lines or by folding the paper into three equal sections). Have your child color the top section red, the middle section black, and the bottom section green to create his own Kwanzaa flag.

Menorah

A menorah consists of nine candles, one for each day of Hanukkah, and one, called the shammash, used to light the other candles.

9 empty thread spools
Playdough
Large birthday candles
Aluminum foil (optional)

Make a Hanukkah menorah using nine empty thread spools to hold the candles. If the candles are a little loose, use some playdough to make them fit snugly. If you want to make the menorah more festive, cover the spools with aluminum foil.

Since a menorah can be any shape or size, use your imagination. Your preschooler can insert candles into playdough or modeling clay that he has shaped into a pleasing design. Try standing candles in a shoebox lid filled with sand, or drill holes for the candles in a tree branch or an interesting piece of driftwood.

Note: Traditionally, you should light your menorah every day and use new candles each time. You will need forty-four candles in total for each menorah you light. Special packages of Hanukkah candles are available during this time of year.

Potato Latkes

Since oil was an important part of the Temple rededication, eating foods cooked in oil has come to symbolize the victory of the Jews over their enemies. This recipe will make about fifteen latkes (Yiddish for "pancake").

Ingredients	Materials
5 medium potatoes	Grater
1 small onion	Medium bowl
2 eggs, beaten	Sieve (to drain potatos)
2 tablespoons flour	Large frying pan
½ teaspoon salt	Slotted spatula
¼ teaspoon pepper	Tablespoon
Salad oil	

1. Grate the potatoes and onion and press out the extra liquid.
2. Add the beaten eggs to the potato/onion mixture.
3. Add the flour, salt, and pepper; mix well.
4. Pour about ¼-inch salad oil into the bottom of a large frying pan. Heat the oil, and keep it hot at medium to medium-high heat. Be careful—the oil will splatter.
5. Put batter by the tablespoon into the oil and press each with a slotted spatula to make a thin pancake.
6. When the edges get brown, turn the latke over and cook the other side until golden brown and crisp.
7. Serve warm with sour cream and applesauce.

Appendix
Basic Craft Recipes

"There is so much to teach, and the time goes so fast."
—*Erma Bombeck*

Even at a very young age, your child can begin to develop her own creative skills and understand the artistic work of others. Visual art is not limited to paper and paint, but includes many different media. The craft materials in this section are essential for every child's artwork: paint, glue, paste, modeling compounds, and more.

PAINT

Each of the following recipes will produce a good paint for your child to use. Each varies in the ingredients required and the method used, so choose one that best suits the supplies you have on hand and the time you have available.

When mixing paint, keep in mind the age of the artist; as a general rule, the younger the artist, the thicker the paint (and brushes) should be. Paint should be stored covered; small plastic spill-proof paint containers are available at your local art supply store. These come with an airtight lid for storage, hold brushes upright nicely without tipping, and, at several dollars each, are well worth the purchase price.

Flour-Based Poster Paint

¼ cup flour
Saucepan
1 cup water
Small jars or plastic containers
3 tablespoons powdered tempera paint
2 tablespoons water
½ teaspoon liquid starch or liquid detergent (optional)

Measure flour into a saucepan. Slowly add 1 cup water to make the paste smooth. Heat, stirring constantly, until mixture begins to thicken. Cool. Measure a quarter cup of the flour paste into a small jar or plastic container. Add three tablespoons powdered tempera paint and two tablespoons water for each color. For an opaque finish, add liquid starch. For a glossy finish, add liquid detergent. Store covered.

Condensed Milk Paint

Bowl or other container
1 cup condensed milk
Food coloring

In a bowl, mix one cup of condensed milk with drops of food coloring to make a very glossy, brightly colored paint. This paint is not intended to be eaten, but it won't harm any child who decides to make a snack of it.

Egg Yolk Paint

This recipe is suitable for painting edible cookies.

1 egg yolk
¼ teaspoon water
Food coloring
Bowl or other container
Paintbrush

In a bowl, mix one egg yolk with a quarter teaspoon water and lots of food coloring. Use a paintbrush to paint freshly baked cookies; return cookies to oven until egg solidifies.

Detergent Poster Paint

1 tablespoon clear liquid detergent
2 teaspoons powdered tempera paint
Small jars or plastic containers

For each color, mix together liquid detergent and powdered tempera paint in a amall jar or plastic container. This makes enough for one painting session.

Homemade Face Paint

This face paint is suitable for painting designs with a small brush.

Bowl or other container
1 teaspoon cornstarch
½ teaspoon cold cream
½ teaspoon water
Food coloring
Small paintbrush

In a bowl, stir together cornstarch and cold cream until well blended. Add water and stir. Add food coloring, one drop at a time until you get the desired color. Paint designs on face with a small paintbrush; remove with soap and water. Store paint in a covered plastic container or a baby food jar.

Halloween Face Paint

Bowl or other container
1 tablespoon solid shortening
2 tablespoons cornstarch
Food coloring
Sponge (optional)
Small paintbrush (optional)

In a bowl, mix shortening and cornstarch together until smooth. Add food coloring, one drop at a time, until you get the desired color. Use a sponge or your fingers to apply paint over a large area, such as an entire face. To paint a design with a small brush, thin the paint with a little water first. Remove with soap and water. Store paint in a baby food jar or a covered plastic container.

FINGERPAINT

Each of the following recipes produces a good
fingerpaint, however the ingredients and mixing
methods vary. Choose one that is suitable for the
ingredients you have on hand and the time you
have available.

Cornstarch Fingerpaint

3 tablespoons sugar
½ cup cornstarch
Medium saucepan
2 cups cold water
Muffin tin or small cups
Spoon
Food coloring
Soap flakes or liquid dishwashing detergent

Mix sugar and cornstarch in a medium saucepan
over low heat. Add cold water and continue stirring
until the mixture is thick. Remove from heat.
Divide the mixture into four or five portions,
spooning them into sections of a muffin tin or
small cups. Add a drop or two of food coloring
and a pinch of soap flakes or a drop of liquid
dishwashing detergent to each portion. Use a
different color for each cup. Stir and let cool.
Store covered in an airtight container.

Flour Fingerpaint

1 cup flour
2 tablespoons salt
1½ cups cold water
1¼ cups hot water
Saucepan
Whisk or rotary beater
Food coloring or powdered tempera paint

Put flour and salt in a saucepan. Add cold water and beat with a whisk or rotary beater until smooth. Add hot water and boil until mixture is thick. Beat again until smooth. Keep in the refrigerator and color as needed with food coloring or powdered tempera paint.

PLAYDOUGH

Everyone seems to have their own favorite playdough recipe, and many old favorites have been included here. Some require cooking, some are no-cook, some are meant to be eaten, and some are not. Choose the recipe that best suits your requirements and the ingredients you have on hand. Store playdough in a covered container or plastic bag. If it sweats a little, just add more flour.

Oatmeal Playdough

This is an ideal playdough for your child to make herself. It must be refrigerated, and it doesn't last as long as cooked playdough.

   1 part flour
   1 part water
   2 parts oatmeal
   Bowl

Combine all ingredients in a bowl; mix well and knead until smooth. This is not intended to be edible, but it will not hurt kids if they eat it.

Colored Playdough

1 cup water
1 tablespoon vegetable oil
½ cup salt
1 tablespoon cream of tartar
Food coloring
Saucepan
1 cup flour

Combine water, oil, salt, cream of tartar, and food coloring in a saucepan and heat until warm. Remove from heat and add flour. Stir, then knead until smooth. Keep in mind that the cream of tartar makes this dough long-lasting—up to six months or longer—so resist the temptation to leave it out if you don't have it on hand. This dough should be stored in an airtight container or a Ziploc bag. Do not refrigerate.

Salt Playdough

1 cup salt
1 cup water
½ cup flour
Saucepan

Combine salt, water, and flour in a saucepan; mix and cook over medium heat. Remove from heat when mixture is thick and rubbery. As the mixture cools, knead in enough flour to make the dough workable.

Peanut Butter Playdough

Definitely an edible playdough!
18 ounces peanut butter
6 tablespoons honey
Nonfat dry milk or milk plus flour
Cocoa or carob for chocolate flavor (optional)
Bowl
Edible treats for decoration

Combine all ingredients in a bowl and mix, adding enough dry milk or milk plus flour to reach the consistency of bread dough. Add cocoa or carob, if desired. Shape, decorate with other edible treats, and eat!

Kool-Aid Playdough

½ cup salt
2 cups water
Saucepan
Food coloring, tempera powder, or Kool-Aid for color
2 tablespoons salad oil
2 cups sifted flour
2 tablespoons alum (available at your grocery or
*   drugstore)*

Boil salt in water in a saucepan until the salt dissolves.
Remove from heat and tint with food coloring,
tempera powder, or Kool-Aid. Add salad oil, flour,
and alum. Knead or process until smooth. This
dough will last two months or longer.

Uncooked Playdough

1 cup cold water
1 cup salt
2 teaspoons vegetable oil
Tempera paint or food coloring
3 cups flour
2 tablespoons cornstarch
Bowl

Mix water, salt, oil, and enough tempera paint to make a bright color. Gradually add flour and cornstarch until the mixture reaches the consistency of bread dough.

CLAY

Use the following recipes to produce clay that can be rolled or shaped into ornaments. The drying methods vary, either overnight or in the oven. When hard, ornaments can be painted and preserved with acrylic.

No-Bake Cookie Clay

These ornaments are not edible!
  2 cups salt
  ⅔ cup water
  Medium saucepan
  1 cup cornstarch
  ½ cup cold water
  Rolling pin
  Cookie cutters
  Straw
  Paint, glitter, and other decorative materials

Mix salt with ⅔ cup water in a medium saucepan. Stir and boil. Add cornstarch and ½ cup cold water and stir. If the mixture doesn't get thick, set it back on the stove. Sprinkle some extra cornstarch onto the table, roll out the dough with a rolling pin, and cut with cookie cutters. Use a straw to make a hole at the top for hanging. Dry and decorate with paint, glitter, and so on.

No-Bake Craft Clay

1 cup cornstarch
1¼ cups cold water
2 cups baking soda (1 pound)
Saucepan
Food coloring (optional)
Plate
Damp cloth
Tempera paints or acrylic paints (optional)
Shellac, clear acrylic, or clear nail polish

Combine cornstarch, cold water, and baking soda in a saucepan; stir over medium heat for about four minutes until the mixture thickens to a moist mashed-potato consistency. For color, add a few drops of food coloring to the water before it is mixed with the starch and soda. Remove from heat, turn out onto a plate and cover with a damp cloth until cool. Knead as you would dough. Shape as desired or store in an airtight container or plastic bag. Objects may be left to dry then painted with tempera paints or acrylics. Dip in shellac, spray with clear acrylic, or brush with clear nail polish to seal.

Baker's Clay

4 cups flour
1 cup salt
1 teaspoon powdered alum
1½ cups water
Food coloring (optional)
Large bowl
Cookie sheet
Cookie cutters (optional)
Plastic straw (optional)
Fine wire (optional)
Fine sandpaper
Plastic-based poster paint, acrylic paint, or markers
Clear shellac, acrylic spray, or clear nail polish

Mix all ingredients in a large bowl. If the dough is too dry, work in another tablespoon of water with your hands. Dough can be colored by dividing it into several parts and kneading a drop or two of food coloring into each part. Roll or mold as desired.

To roll: Roll dough one-eighth-inch thick on a lightly floured surface. Cut with cookie cutters dipped in flour. Make a hole in the top, quarter-inch down, for hanging, by using the end of a plastic straw dipped in flour. Shake the dots of clay from the straw and press onto the dough shape as decorations.

To mold: Shape dough no more than half-inch thick into figures, such as flowers, fruits, animals, and so on. Insert a fine wire in each for hanging.

Bake ornaments on an ungreased cookie sheet for about thirty minutes in a 250 degree oven. Turn and bake another one and a half hours until hard and dry. Remove and cool, then sand lightly with fine sandpaper until smooth. Paint both sides with plastic-based poster paint, acrylic paint, or markers. Allow paint to dry and seal with clear shellac, acrylic spray, or clear nail polish.

Makes about five dozen two-and-a-half-inch ornaments.

Modeling Clay

2 cups salt
⅔ cups water
Saucepan
1 cup cornstarch
½ cup cold water

Stir salt and water in a saucepan over heat four to five minutes. Remove from heat; add cornstarch and cold water. Stir until smooth; return to heat and cook until thick. Store in a plastic bag.

Bread Clay

6 slices white bread
6 tablespoons white glue
½ teaspoon detergent or 2 teaspoons glycerin
Food coloring
Paintbrush
Acrylic paints, acrylic spray, or clear nail polish

Remove the crusts from white bread and knead the
bread with glue plus either detergent or glycerin
until the mixture is no longer sticky. Separate into
portions and tint with food coloring. Let your child
shape the clay. Brush the finished product with
equal parts glue and water for a smooth appearance.
Let dry overnight to harden. Use acrylic paints,
acrylic spray, or clear nail polish to seal and preserve.

GLUE and PASTE

The following glue and paste recipes use a variety of ingredients and methods. Choose the one that best suits your project. For variety, add food coloring to glue before using. Store all products in airtight containers in the refrigerator.

No-Cook Paste

½ cup flour
Water
Salt
Bowl

Mix flour with water until gooey. Add a pinch of salt; stir.

Glue

¾ cup water
2 tablespoons corn syrup
1 teaspoon white vinegar
Small saucepan
Small bowl
2 tablespoons cornstarch
¾ cup cold water

Mix water, corn syrup, and white vinegar in a small saucepan. Bring to a full, rolling boil. In a small bowl, mix cornstarch with cold water. Add this mixture slowly to the hot mixture, stirring constantly until the mixture returns to a boil. Boil for one minute, then remove from heat. When slightly cooled, pour into another container and let stand overnight before using.

Homemade Paste

½ cup flour
Cold water
Saucepan
Flavoring and/or food coloring (optional)

Add some cold water to the flour until it is as thick as cream. Simmer and stir in a saucepan for five minutes. Add a few drops of flavoring and/or food coloring, if desired. This recipe makes a wet, messy paste that takes a while to dry.

Papier-Mâché Paste

1 cup water
¼ cup flour
5 cups lightly boiling water
Large saucepan

Mix flour into one cup of water until the mixture is thin and runny. Stir this mixture into the lightly boiling water. Gently boil and stir for two to three minutes. Cool before using.

OTHER CRAFT RECIPES

Use the following recipes to make interesting materials for use in various arts and crafts projects.

Pasta Dye

½ cup rubbing alcohol
Food coloring
Bowl
Variety of dry pasta
Newspapers
Wax paper
Spoon

Mix alcohol and food coloring in a bowl. Add small amounts of various dry pasta to the liquid and gently mix. The larger the pasta, the longer it will take to absorb the color. Dry on newspapers covered with wax paper.

Egg Dye

¼ teaspoon food coloring
¾ cup hot water
1 tablespoon white vinegar
Bowl or cup
Eggs

Measure all liquids into a bowl or a cup and mix.
Use different food coloring in each container for
desired shades. Soak eggs in the dyes until they
reach the desired shades.

Colorful Creative Salt

½ cup salt
5 to 6 drops food coloring
Wax paper or microwave-safe container and microwave

Add food coloring to salt and stir well. Cook in a
microwave for one to two minutes, or spread on
wax paper and let air dry. Store in an airtight
container. Use as you would glitter.

Ornamental Frosting

This frosting works like an edible glue; use for
gingerbread houses or other food projects that
you want to eat!

  3 egg whites
  1 teaspoon cream of tartar
  1 pound powdered sugar, sifted (about 4 cups)
  Bowl
  Egg beater
  Damp cloth

Beat egg whites with cream of tartar in a bowl until
stiff peaks form. Add sifted icing sugar and continue
beating until mixture is thick and holds its shape.
Cover with a damp cloth when not in use. This
mixture can be made several hours or the day
before using. Store in an airtight container in
the refrigerator.